Narrow Bridge

OTHER BOOKS BY
BARBARA PELMAN

Aubade Amalfi
(Rubicon Press, 2016)

Borrowed Rooms
(Ronsdale Press, 2008)

One Stone
(Ekstasis Editions, 2005)

narrow
bridge

Barbara Pelman

[handwritten signature: Pelman]

[handwritten inscription: love to Barbara — Partners in crime, in poetry, in name! More to come, eh? Barbara Nov 2017]

RONSDALE

NARROW BRIDGE
Copyright © 2017 Barbara Pelman

RONSDALE PRESS
3350 West 21st Avenue
Vancouver, B.C., Canada V6S 1G7
www.ronsdalepress.com

Typesetting: Julie Cochrane, in New Baskerville 11 pt on 13.5
Cover Design: Julie Cochrane
Paper: Enviro 100 Edition, 55 lb. Enviro Antique Cream (FSC) —
    100% post-consumer waste, totally chlorine-free and acid-free

Ronsdale Press wishes to thank the following for their support of its publishing
program: the Canada Council for the Arts, the Government of Canada through
the Canada Book Fund, the British Columbia Arts Council, and the Province
of British Columbia through the Book Publishing Tax Credit Program.

Library and Archives Canada Cataloguing in Publication

Pelman, Barbara, author
   Narrow bridge / Barbara Pelman.

Poems.

Issued in print and electronic formats.
ISBN 978-1-55380-508-3 (softcover)
ISBN 978-1-55380-509-0 (ebook) / ISBN 978-1-55380-510-6 (pdf)

   I. Title.

PS8631.E4685.N37 2017   C811'.6   C2017-903926-1   C2017-903927-X

At Ronsdale Press we are committed to protecting the environment. To this
end we are working with Canopy and printers to phase out our use of paper
produced from ancient forests. This book is one step towards that goal.

Printed in Canada by Marquis Book Printing, Quebec

for Lara,
Annie,
and Jed

ACKNOWLEDGEMENTS

I would like to thank Rubicon Press for permission to use the following poems which are part of the chapbook *Aubade Amalfi: the Marcello Poems* (2016): "Aubade at Amalfi," "Marcello's Feet," "First Lesson," "Postcard from Ischia," "Why She Went to Italy," and "The Better Story." And thank you to the Federation of BC Writers *WordWorks* journal for permission to use the poem "Aubade Amalfi" which won first prize in the Literary Writes Contest 2014. Also thanks to Leaf Press, who published the following poems in the Honeymoon Bay series from the Patrick Lane retreats: "Marcello's Feet" (2013), "The Painting" (2016), "Wabi-Sabi" (2016); to Caitlin Press, who published "Tashlik" in the anthology *Refugium* (2017); and to the following magazines in which these poems first appeared: "Raspberries, Regret" (*CV2*, 2015), "Thisness" (*Freefall*, 2012), "Walking the Dog" (*Passages North*, 2012), "Between Your Heartbeats" (*Arc Poetry* "Reader's Choice," 2011), "The Better Story" (*Freefall*, 2013).

My thanks to Russell Thorburn, for endless rejigging of these pages, and for his wise organization; to Ron Hatch, who persevered with this manuscript and previous manifestations of it, and to all at Ronsdale Press for beautiful books.

Thanks also to Patrick Lane, whose retreats at Glenairley, then Ocean Wilderness, and now at Honeymoon Bay were terrifyingly marvellous. He guided many of these poems through the rigors of cadence, rhyme, punctuation, line and syntax with affectionate firmness and perceptiveness.

I am grateful to the Waywords, who have met for the past fourteen years to write and edit and support, and to all my poetry friends who have graciously edited poems, talked poetry, written poems with me, particularly Susan Stenson, Yvonne Blomer and Arleen Pare, early editors of this book. Finally, to my family in Vancouver, my intrepid hundred-year-old mother, and most of all, to my beautiful family in Sweden, all my love and gratitude.

"All the world is a narrow bridge —
the important thing is not to be afraid at all."
— RABBI NACHMAN OF BRESLOV

CONTENTS

– I –

-I-

Gentle Reader

based on the painting by Karen Hollingsworth

There is a breeze off the sea, you can tell from the curtains,
though the colours tell you that too. If you were sitting
in the white wicker chair, your hair would move a little,
you would brush away a strand, settle deeper
into the pillows. A rhythm of waves
at the shoreline, the steady beat
entering the room. A chair, some books,
a window.

       What is outside this room?
Nothing beyond the words on the page,
the water's percussion, an echo of the concerto
you listened to this morning.

Look again.
       How long can you live here,
before longing enters — that hillside in Sicily,
those buildings in Riga —
where can you be that fills you up again and again?

If only you believed this were enough —
this pillow behind your back, this book,
the sea beyond you. The wind.

Any Morning

Waking up, those moments when the day
or the month or the year is lost
in the threads of a dream — an attic room,
an old lover, a red truck.

And the day opens slowly, unfolds its hours
without lists of things you need to do —
no papers in neat piles to mark, no clothes
to wash other than your own.

It could be Monday, it could be winter,
it doesn't matter. The sun is somewhere
you can find, the sea is waiting,
even the rain, something skin can love.

The one who judges you still sleeps. The mother
you have eaten has lost her voice. It's dark
inside you, and quiet. Nothing is being said
you need deny.

Raspberries, Regret

starting with a line from Gwendolyn MacEwen

And think of nothing else but raspberries
cold with rain, magnolia full of stars,
hummingbird returning to the branches —
think of nothing else, clear the clotted mind
and name each moment that flickers on the nerve:
this is merely regret, this
is murderous rage, this is confusion.
Name it and let it go, a feather's touch
against your skin, nothing there to hurt you.
Think of willows bending to the river,
the river running between green banks,
think of raspberries in a yellow bowl,
nothing else but raspberries, heavy with cream.

Gifts

The sky is brilliant today,
the trees blaze their dead leaves
in gold and crimson, an ecstasy
of mourning. How is it that death
is so beautiful? The skeletons
of trees on the seashore, the small jewels
of insects caught in the spiderweb, the wing
of a robin, perfectly spread on the pavement.
The grey days will come, but for now
we study how to deserve

all this light. It's not that we've been good —
sheltered the homeless, fed
the hungry, laid down our weapons
or cleaned our watersheds. It's not
that we trained our children well or forgave
our parents — we still treasure
the recipe for rage we sometimes offered
our husbands. And yet
this amazing day, our cherished hearts —
what has already been given us.

Leaving

a cento

The melon scent of you
lingers in the corridor, in the linen.

There is no other way for us.

Were you to go
I'd sleep in every elsewhere,
would pack a bag
and book passage with the ferryman,
his bag of coins, his indifference.

Doors open outward,
coffins close.

Maybe I'll care tomorrow.
There is a happy stranger somewhere inside me.

Piano Lesson

Not all things are blest, but the
seeds of all things are blest.
— Muriel Rukeyser, "Elegy in Joy"

The Nordheimer piano, bought at an auction —
dark wood, scratched in places,
ivory keys, surprisingly in tune
after all the years and distance.
Even a piano bench
full of music, someone who loved it.

My fingers remember scales
from sixty years ago. Sharps and flats,
arpeggios. Left hand awkward,
right hand clumsy, brain struggles
to read the score, listen, remember, learn.
What I remember one minute
I forget the next. Rhythm and cadence,
metronome beats steadily, staccato,
pause, cacophony of wrong notes:
But no one here to censure or mock
my fumbling practice.

From brain to hands, trust
where the fingers go,
slide into the melody, let it flow
through bone and muscle.
Play with your whole arms,
someone tells me. I watch Rubinstein
and Gould online, their body
tuned to the music.

Why begin, so late? Re-create myself,
another chance to be what I haven't been —
and this quiet groping at midnight,
dissonant sounds, swiftly corrected,
over and over until the fingers know their place,
Beethoven's Ode to Joy —
one clear note after the other.

Blue Moon

And I have nothing to offer you now
save my own wild emptiness.
— Cecilia Woloch, "Grace"

The summer begins to cool,
I wrap a shawl around my evenings.
Have you seen the blue moon?

To love what does not last — bright grief.
Offer anything to avoid this truth,
my favourite book, my best art, my first-born.

Sit at the window as the moon slides behind the hills —
open your hands and catch the wind,
feel its weight on your palm.

Your silver and gold, your careful words,
the gifts I lay at your feet — nothing
to be held or passed on. Stardust on the window pane.

Hands empty in the cooling mornings,
wild at twilight.

The Basket

after Mary Ruefle's "The Cart"

Somewhere a woman carries a basket on her head,
humming. It might be the day her daughter is to be married,
the day her chickens have died, the fields have dried up.
How can she signal her acceptance of this world? What if
a scorpion lights on her arm? Its deadly tail
whipping the wind. She reaches up,
allowing the scorpion to settle in the basket. She carries him
as she carries the husband who neglects her, the harvest
that withers, the body of a child unwilling to be born.

Loosely Held

They will not come again, those boys
I so easily lay down for, those break-free days,
and with no mother's admonitions in my head
I could say yes, and yes, and yes. They will not come
these winter days, those lingering boys in their sweaters
and sneakers, who parked their VW vans in the driveway.
And I, weightless, drifted from door to door to door
carrying stones from the river to hold me down.
Where are they now, those summer boys? Fathers
and grandfathers, reminiscing on porches. Two by two
into the ark, couples now shredding, shedding mortgages
and separating dishes, couches, pictures. The sweaters
frayed, vans sold, stones cold and heavy in my hands.

Something That Arrives After

It's August and the garden is full of roses. When rain falls,
she walks the side roads, picks blackberries.
Passes a deer, its head raised, ears swivelling.
She is learning to draw and paint, has taken up the flute.
If a man speaks love after all these years,
and leaves, what does it say about patience?
She makes blackberry pies, feeds herself, gives
to the neighbours. She is at the beginning after the end,
the road unsure and full of pebbles. Danger everywhere
and dazzling. The air warm and drizzled,
the blackberries, summer in her mouth.

The Angel of Silence

The angel waits, as she always does,
on the doorstep, the door closed

in front of her. Before the knock,
before the bell, the unexpected letter

through the mail slot. All possibility
in her pocket.

Between piano keys,
pause as the fingers lift, the chord —

G minor, filling the galaxies,
sliding under her spacious wings.

She guards wisdom
against ephemera, stands at the gate

where words spill, too easy —
not yet the right ones. If she could speak,

listen, she would say. Wait.

She is the first breath, before the cry,
before the first word: *Bereishit.*

We could call her *Aleph,*
where language begins.

Bereishit: the first word in the Bible, "the beginning."

Thisness

This winter afternoon while others work
she sits on the veranda and rests —
she does not move inside
where there is warmth and no hunger.

She rests, and wonders,
lets the cold shiver her;
she does not mind; what the cold does
is good. She feels her body — legs, arms, belly —
not just thinks it, the way her mind always
will search for the word before the feeling.
But not today.

Today she wants emptiness.
Hunts for it, though she knows
that's not the way to find it:
not the endless and futile searching
for a peace that hunger cannot touch.
Happiness, fed from detail: the *thisness* of things,
resting in the eye of the beetle, the creak of the board
she leans against, the cold air pricking her ears.

Bowl of Light

for Phyllis

The bowl sits in the middle of the table.
It is large enough to nestle a cat,
a dozen apples, bathwater for a baby.
Today it is empty, curling around air,
waiting to be filled, or not.
The bowl is blue — summer-sky blue,
delphinium blue, forget-me-not blue.
It holds memories of pasta served in the galley
that winter we lived on the boat,
rowed to shore and into the car
and down the highway to work.
It remembers summers filled with crab casserole,
a dozen crowded around a table,
tanned cheeks and hands scented with seaweed.
It has held Christmas balls made from ashes
of St. Helens, swirls of blue and green.
The flames from the fireplace
throw slivers of light onto the blue.
I hold the bowl in both hands,
offer its emptiness to the morning sun
that stripes the cloud, silhouettes the maple.
Offer emptiness to the day's clockwork,
a pause in the pendulum's heavy beat.

Stagnant Hour

Midnight. The waning moon
rises above the cedar,
sketch of tree on the rocks below.
A man stands by the window,
the moon on his cheek.
He is not thinking, only listening
to the sound of cars
in the street below. The roses
he sent her, returned,
droop their musky scent on the table
where he has left them, still wrapped.
Roses will not cancel words said,
she wrote him. And that was that.
This is not a house, but a stagnant hour,
the walls dull stone, the ceiling
a weight above his head, like the caves
they twisted through last summer, their voices
echoing, words in a dream,
the tang of fear a sharpness in his throat,
the stone walls squeezing and kneading
like rough hands on bread. He would never
be born again in such darkness, never
rise to light and air, the smell of roses
crushed, the moon about to fall.

The Well

How easily the words come out wrong.
You dip into the well of language and pull up
scorpions. You never meant it,
you don't know what happened, you lowered the bucket
and your mother came up, spouting platitudes
and judgment. You can't burn her, or hide her in a cave
and heap up stones. You can't bury her
in an unmarked grave. She will lay down seeds,
they will wait for rain, they will grow immense:
Amorphophallus titanum:
corpse flowers.

Between Your Heartbeats

Here, where you are, there's room
between your heartbeats,
as if everything you have ever been
begins, inside, to sing.
— Lorna Crozier, "A Summer's Singing"

I wonder what that's like,
to come to a place of knowing,
to feel, *I have been here,* or
this is where I belong —
to open a door not yours
but not unfamiliar,
to place a hand on a chair
and know there is nowhere else to go:
a fairy tale or a lucky ticket?
Here, where you are, there's room

even the smallest room, to consider:
the Kabbalists call it *simcha:*
joy unattended by cause,
merely being, in sun or snow,
the light after the storm.
Not searching for it, but perhaps ready,
already there, the morning sun
like a blessing, everything
a blessing, and
between your heartbeats

the breath. One step
in front of the other, like headlights
on a dark night, darkness flung
by light, a little at a time.
Still, there are the old myths you believe in:
someone by your side —
helpmeet, soulmate, Adam and maiden,
and how to rewrite? Erase
and revise, make it your story,
as if everything you have ever been

was reaching for this place of knowing.
To want it all is to choose
nothing. The days gather into a glowering,
winter dark falls early: in the grate,
a fire caught in its nest of wood.
The unfilled hollow
at the base of the throat, a calling
and a silence, the music everywhere
if you listen, and your voice, finally,
begins, inside, to sing.

Salt

i

Eight hundred stairs down,
the Wieliczka Salt Mines, Krakow.
We touch our fingers to the walls,
lick them. In crevices and along the path,
salt sculptures of bearded men,
backs bent to shovels of salt,
picks cracking the walls, and horses
who never knew sunlight
trudge beside them. A thousand metres under.
No wonder the need for the huge cathedral,
even the frieze of the Last Supper formed
from salt. And the four chandeliers,
teardrops of salt, hanging long shadows on the walls.
Ancient seas dried and buried underground,
sodium chloride, worth its weight in gold.
Thousands of tons of salt
crossing the desert in camel caravans,
salt roads across the Mediterranean.

ii

Throw salt over your shoulder to ward off evil spirits,
sprinkle your offerings with salt. Salt the Sabbath challah
and the newborn to keep him safe. My grandson,
no longer a newborn, bounces on his mother's back,
leans to the walls to taste salt.

iii

Sometimes it seems the ones you love most
are the most difficult to talk to.
Salt in old wounds. A pinch of salt
to cleanse the broken places.
My tongue stumbles on words weighed,
measured, examined. *Let your conversation
be always full of grace, seasoned with salt"*
(St. Paul). Where is the grace?

iv

We find our way slowly upward,
past a lake saturated with salt, emerald
and hidden. *Crystal Grotto.* Walls of salt,
long passageways we stumble into,
then a small cage hauls us to the surface.
In a few weeks, I will return home,
say farewell to daughter, grandson,
words still crystallized in my mouth.

v

A thousand metres underground.
Light filters through the saturated lake,
echoes darkly on the salt figures,
the salt walls. We dig deep
to find such light, search for truth
our tongues can hold, carve cathedrals
out of what we find there, grace
seasoned with salt.

Autumn Equinox

The day balances on the equator
and falls toward darkness. Soon the rain —
the percussioned roof, a relentless companion.
Our summer skin hidden under layers of wool.
What is open to the wind and rain gathers a strength
that summer knows nothing of. Rain
along the seashore, the horizon hazy and grey,
only a breath between earth and sky.
Along the shore a lone crow shivers,
sprays dark rain into the haze.
The air is cupped with sound
of gull and wind. What proliferates
in the places that close?
The maple's green hands bend
into a winter fist.

Elegy

So much goes unnoticed: the blue jay new to the oak
outside the window, red leaf in November rain,
a moment of clear sky. I leave the radio on,
so that music meets me at the door: a cello sonata,

a Bach fugue, a bit of Gershwin. I am learning
the difference between major and minor,
progressions and arpeggios. The jay calls a C note
I think, test it on the piano, newly tuned.

It's the weather untunes it, my teacher tells me,
and the sky suddenly seems larger, enters
my small rooms, the strings of my body.
In the garden, the oak drops its seeds,

squirrels fill their cheeks, the leaves shrivel,
the sky closes. Beethoven, C minor
through the open window, the jay stops, listens,
blue head cocked, black eyes catching mine.

Even Now

after Rita Dove's "Borderline Mambo"

As if you could get the pickle jar to open.
As if you could find an ice cream seller
who didn't give you soft ice cream and say
it was the same as hard, the real stuff. As if
everything good to eat didn't have something in it
that would kill you, as if those numbers on the glucometer
made a difference to your quality of life. As if
you could plié again, hand on the wooden barre,
Shostakovich on the CD player, bend, rise, balance.
Three years of dance classes in your sixties,
what you could no longer do
but could remember from your childhood —
the empty studio, grand jetés across the floor,
your image gliding in the mirror. Lift. Turn. Spot.
Leap. And though your new knees could barely manage it,
those same jetés you performed
down the hallways of the surgeon's office.
What can still be done, do it. The rented cello
in the corner of the room, the piano in the parlour,
the flute in its velvet bed. Make music,
even now. Eat ice cream every chance you get
despite the numbers on the dial. Make pickles
the way your mother did, sing the songs
your father sang to you, driving in the car
down roads that are now highways. Gershwin,
Verdi, the liturgy from Sabbath services.
As if choice is a simple thing, this or that.

Bridges

i

I cast out language, word after word,
like a small bridge
across a wide river.

ii

The bridge is up. Why go anywhere?
There is nothing you can take home
in your melting hands.

iii

Which to prefer?
The thrill of uncertainty,
the comfort of return:
the first step onto the bridge,
or the last.

iv

Stranger, do you not see?
This brick in my hand
can build bridges.

v

Standing in the middle of the bridge,
three choices:
Go back. Go forward.
Jump.

- II -

Why She Went to Italy

Because her poems had become crowded
with Garry oak and daffodils
and one hummingbird in the hawthorn

Because nobody asked her to
or told her to
or suggested she should

Because when two trains going in opposite directions
are on the same track and everyone shrugs and says,
"That's Italy" — it's an acceptable answer

And she wanted to learn
how to lift her shoulders —
that slow, articulate shrug

Because the hedges
on the side of the narrow roads in Forio
are jasmine

Because of clay-caked hands
and long strands of pasta
and a pair of red Italian sandals

Because "solo" can be sung
in fortissimo
and in crescendo

Because an empty space
invites a vase of tulips
or a stranger named Paolo

And because of what the morning sun
on a tiled patio
overlooking the blue Tyrrhenian Sea
can do to the four chambers
of the human heart.

The Painting

She wants so many things . . .
To walk by the seashore near her home
and count waves, like the woman at Willows Beach,
skirt tucked up in dhoti-fashion,
white haired and barefoot,
a small dog beside her, sniffing the seaweed,

or to be gazing at Titian's *Venus of Urbino*
in Florence, the bold stare
so unlike her own diffidence, preferring her
to the blue-robed Madonnas in their cumbersome folds,
and she wishes she too were waiting for her lover,
body gleaming as if oiled and scented.

But what if this Venus is planning to leave him,
her trunk already packed, a letter propped on the mantel —
no, maybe not a letter, no goodbyes —
the servants folding the last garment, the silk smock
she will wear in her studio,
(he never asks about her studio, or her work)

and she will cut her red hair,
tuck her smock into a pair of borrowed pants,
and when her painting is finished,
she will open the doors to the Umbrian breeze,
walk by the seashore, skipping stones,
singing a tune she has just composed.

Postcard from Ischia

The road snakes in and around the hills,
like a lover returning again and again
to his desire. Far below, the sea —
above, clear sky — both the colour
we call Mediterranean.
Jasmine fills the air — small white clusters
in a bowl of green, and lemon trees,
like a yellow knife to the senses.
Down the hill, stone walls
merely an arm's stretch apart,
fields of tomato and garlic and grape —
a rooster crows the morning awake,
announces the weather:
no rain today, no wind either.

If you were here, we'd walk the shore,
gather clams and mussels for pasta —
rigatoni, tagliatelle, gnocchi —
and we'd wind our way up the hill
sun-struck and wind-washed,
listen to the village sounds muffled
by pine and poplar, look out over the wrinkled sea.
We'd throw away our travel books,
kick off our new Italian shoes,
change our address: Top of the Hill,
Ischia, Italy.

All of It Overflowing

The sky is heavy and full of rain,
maple leaves scatter the driveway,
hump in heaps on the lawn.
Bushes straggle, weeds like tattered rags
along the fence where the squirrel
stops, listening. It is the time
before the time of silence,
before the clean lines of bare branch,
before whiteness.

This windy abundance — weed and leaf,
thick cloud and buckets of rain,
we need the time to gather wood,
lay our fires, stir the soup pot,
prepare our hibernations. Soon enough
the land will be empty, doors will close,
we will walk our internal landscapes
as the days tighten from dark to dark.
There, by the fire, we will imagine

headlong tumble of water from mountain snow,
kaleidoscope of colour in back gardens,
heliotrope and fuchsia, apple blossoms —
all possibility in one green leaf,
and the circle of sky, blue and shining,
sun on skin, wind a tangle
in hair and treetops. Each day,
a little more light, we run,
angled toward blessing.

Impression, Sunrise

after Monet's painting, 1874

Monet called it a *pochade*, a sketch,
a moment transfixed at the end of his brush —
the orange sun, its reflection on the still water,
three boats and a haze of harbour.
One man standing at the stern,
adjusting his eyes to the opening light.
He had crept quietly out of his house,
taking his small son with him.
If they fish today,
they will feast tonight.
The boy catches the rising sun in the water,
cups his hands around the light.
The harbour is silent, only a splash
of oar and one gull overhead.
A moment, an anecdote of light,
everything within the frame:
day and darkness and the thought
of a fish, the sun a bright coin
spilling dinner.

This Not That

Marcello wanders somewhere on the streets of Lucca,
playing his cello to buy sheet music. Elgar, Dvořák, Bach.
My friends wander the streets of Venice, writing poems
full of music: Giudecca, Cannaregio, San Polo.
I've discovered Chopin, pluck his tunes out on the piano,
minus half the notes. It's hard to learn again.

If I were elsewhere, if I had chosen *this* instead of *that*,
a flat in London, Notting Hill, a doctorate,
or a teaching post in the Philippines, Tunisia, Lisbon.
These parallel lives that tantalize, invite envy
as if a distant cousin flaunting his lottery winnings.

How to build a life bereft of the mantras
my mother carved into my veins.
We of the '60s outgrew them,
or so we thought. *A woman without a man
is like a fish without a bicycle.* Brave words.

How the *larghetto*, Chopin's second piano concerto —
adagio of heartbreak, note after quiet note,
and then joy finally, *rondo vivace.* Accept the dance,
he says. Where you are, you are.

I have wandered the streets of London, Forio, Florence:
sycamore, japonica, grey stone and blue tile.
Now, on a street in a small town on the far west coast:
rain, seashore, grey cloud and scent of kelp.

The Better Story

And if there had been a lover,
an old friend she hadn't seen in thirty years
sitting at La Caravelle sipping limoncello —
if she had called his name and he had turned,
and she had gone to his room,
up the maze of tunnelled streets,
through the red door tucked in the shadows —

and if he had taken off all her layers of doubt,
stretched his musician's hands
to the skin of her, and they had spread their lives
on the patio, and he offered her wine
from the steep vineyards of Amalfi,
a little pasta, a long afternoon under the lemon trees,
an orange sunrise over the hills of Capri.

And wasn't this the best of Italy?

And didn't she finally return safe,
a story in her pocket, something to tell her friends —
the smell of lemon and jasmine on the morning wind,
Marcello sipping his espresso, if he was still there,
if he was ever there?

Cornwall

In the morning she sets out, blue pack stuffed with book and
journal, a peach, some crackers. Soft leather sandals bought
in Venice, a short white dress embroidered in blue — a gift
from the lover she had left. The day is ahead of her, and its
silence. She follows the footpaths, past sheep, around cow
patties, over stiles and under fences, climbing the wind-torn
hills. Far below, the tides of the Atlantic scratch the shore.
Wind and sun in her hair, sounds of birds. A hawk hovers,
wings spread in perfect balance: *goshawk* she thinks, somehow
knowing this bird, its effortless riding. She watches, writes,
reads, sitting at the edge of the Cornwall cliffs. Later she will
eat steak in the one good restaurant, and flirt with the waiter.
She is running away, this beautiful place is only temporary.
A plane ticket in her backpack, meetings in September. But
for now, there is nothing else but wind and warm air, the long
footpaths, the basso voices of the sheep, the tenor of the waves,
the stretch of the goshawk's wings.

Nobody knows you here,
all the long day in your hand,
footprints unread.

Café

It is important, sitting at a public café,
a computer in front of you,
to keep your fingers moving.

People will then think you are a writer,
not a dilettante or a philanderer of time.
Keep the small black letters moving

like ants or drizzles of ink across the page,
without photos or videos
decorating the space.

Avoid long lists (diet tips, celebrities who have married
more than five times, names of strange creatures
living in the Mariana Trench) and Buzzfeed.

Scroll through old poems, journals,
and try to ignore the conversation beside you.
Notice the lineup of office workers,

the disappearance of your favourite scone,
the thump of the espresso maker. Don't make a list
of what to do next.

Line by line by line,
a poem stumbles toward a source —
if memory falters, try observation:

the Christmas balls hanging from the lamps,
plump packages of coffee, the pile of newspapers —
check the time again, your new neighbours.

Eavesdropping might start a poem. Listen.
Did you know she was sick? We just saw her
a couple of months ago and now she's gone.

Death and loss, the pendulum of every poem.

Suitcase in the Closet

I'm washing the dishes — the same dishes
I've washed for ten years,
the same dinner as last night,
the same music playing on the stereo.
This is comfort — nothing new
to toss my mind in many directions,
the tiptoe girl who wants only
to know what comes next.
In the painting on the wall, the woman
looks down her nose at me.

There are taverns in Argentina
where they dance the milonga all night.
There is a man, watchful,
looking for the right woman to dance with —
somebody new, a little sparkle on the cold floor.

I put each dish away, clear the table,
set a place for one: coffee cup and breakfast plate
ready for the morning. Perhaps
I'll go out for breakfast —
up the Malahat, on the way to somewhere else.
Perhaps I'll pack a lunch,
see where the day finds me.
The woman in the painting frowns:

A lunch is not far enough. Pack
a suitcase, leave the car at the airport.
They say the light in Greece is like no other light.
It will soften your skin, make your heart strong.

Perhaps tomorrow I will buy
a frisky little skirt, new sandals, some lingerie —
I brush my teeth, pull back the covers,
stretch out in the wide bed. One pillow is enough.

In a tavern on Mykonos, a man sits
drinking ouzo. His wife has died.
All day he offers his boat for tourists.
In the afternoon he reads English books
to improve his mind. He too dreams of a suitcase.

But the day is just another day
and the bed is just a bed,
and the woman, her hair
a cloud around her face, dances
in a tavern somewhere in Argentina —
and the man in Mykonos drinks ouzo
and the boat goes out in the morning
and back every night.

Red Shoes

*based on Hans Christian Andersen's
fairy tale, "The Red Shoes"*

She puts on the red toe shoes, crimson ribbons circling her
ankles, and the shoes dance her through the narrow streets,
the cobbled square with its tall houses, along the canal and
into the park in the middle of the town. They pirouette her
through the forest of birches on the outside of town, jeté her
over fallen branches, meandering roots of oak and maple.
She is happy, she doesn't notice the wind rising, or the shadows
that grow longer as she bourrées between trees, out into the
valley. The hills crowd in on her, her legs tire, but the shoes
keep dancing her beyond the mountains, beyond the villages,
into the dirty streets and out again. She can't stop, she can't
return, the ribbons grip her ankles like chains, the feet in their
relentless red slippers. Is this what love does? What must be
amputated, in order to be free?

First Lesson

Do you remember when we met,
my first class in Italian, that college summer,

and your first time teaching. You brought
Dante's language into the classrooms of Perugia

where you lived and played the streets
with your cello. You had a hat full of coins

and a voice full of music. *Ciao*, you greeted me,
Ciao, I stumbled back. How do you say

your eyes are the dark stars of a million galaxies.
How do you say *your lips are trembling roses.*

How do you say *let me touch that curl of hair*
that falls over your eyes.

Sono felice di incontrarvi,
you say to the class. *Ascolta,* you tell us.

Everyone listens. Here's how to ask for water,
Vorrei un bicchiere d'acqua.

How do you say, *kiss me, Marcello,*
under the olive tree, your Dante tongue

against mine. I will fill your mouth
with the only words I know: grazie. bella. ti amo.

Learning Silence (a fugue)

for my teacher, Gidi, z'l

The summer's last roses, like blown silk against the branches,
leaves shining crimson outside the hospice window.
Can you see the sun? Your family around you.
Nothing is happening except dying.
The days crawling into caverns,
dark at supper, can you see the sun?
Your grandchild learning to speak,
while you learn silence.

The leaves crimson beside the window
far away. Wife, daughter, sister
learning your silence. Summer's late roses
in a vase on the table, petals on the crimson
tablecloth. I sit at home, neither lover
nor daughter nor wife nor sister, I cannot speak.
What words could I offer? The day closes,
the sun crawls into shadows.

Almond

White blossoms by the window, like snow,
and the story we were told: a bride grieving
her northern homeland, her husband
planting almond trees to console her.
Late January, a winter vacation in Portugal.
Two people who seemed to be happy
and why would we not? A house
growing out of a hillside back home,
a daughter safe at college,
a dozen years married. We leaned
against the windowsill, our room
at the edge of town, overlooking the castle.
Narrow streets and whitewashed walls,
honeysuckle in clay pots by the doorsteps.
Behind the walls, courtyards
full of secrets and bougainvillea.
And did the almonds blooming in winter
bring comfort? I think of their bitter core.

Marcello's Feet

I am distracted by the knuckles of his toe,
the arch of his foot against my thigh.
In the bath I wash his feet, slowly,
my fingers between the big toe, the little toe,
soap the instep, the arch, the rough heel,
my hand under the ball
of his foot, stroke, press
and later, on the patio,
his feet against the Roman tiles —
horse and chariot, twining vine leaves.
My feet in his lap —
Ah, he says, his fingers circling my ankle,
little shorn lambs of desire,
as the sun climbs the hills of Positano.

Firenze

For a brief summer
the meandering streets of Florence
were home. No matter

the days were short, eaten by galleries
and leather purses. I feed on memory
the way the streets fed language and footprint.

What in these days of quiet isn't someone's symphony?

Now the streets of Firenze
no longer a feast of cannelloni or statuary,
but something someone else might visit,

spend a few hundred euro
to rent a room overlooking the Arno,
someone who doesn't have a grandson

who reaches out when she comes to visit,
his hands full of peaches, touching her cheek,
his laugh more delicious than gelato,

more heart-filling than the arias of Verdi,
more sumptuous than Titian's Venus
who lounges boldly in the Uffizi

while the blue-robed Madonnas
feed their darling boy.

Dinner

A house with whitewashed walls. A path to the olive trees
and bougainvillea around the doorway. An old dream
dulled now, the way silver loses its shine even
in a dark closet. Perhaps she will write about it,
at least shine the silver and bring out her best cutlery,
set the table for two and see who comes to the door.
She thinks of the old women in tourist buses who
return to the landscapes of lovers, plant coins
and dance with the local men, those with caps raked
across their eyebrows, sandals flapping the floor.
She doesn't believe she is one of these. Not for her
the brief dreams to wrap around a winter night.
She will be the stranger who lives in the villa
on the hilltop, the one with the open windows,
who plants her coins in the olive grove, waters them
with language, who reads her poems in the *taverna*,
the villagers tapping their heels, offering ouzo,
fresh bread, a bowl of green figs.

Go

A woman over seventy should open her travel account,
run her fingers over the globe, and choose

She should trade her sensible shoes for sandals,
her Gucci bag for backpack, her datebook for weather reports

When the sun is in Scorpio, she should sell her stock options,
buy a cottage in Devon, or Bordeaux, or Vilnius

Roads without destination, cafés without tablecloths,
days without a calendar

By the river, by the sea cliff, at the edge of the canal,
over the bridge and through the long tunnels

Her tongue tangling across new syllables
Ears turned to birdsong, accordion, balalaika

click of cicada at sunrise, chitter of leaves in the olive tree,
a stranger's muted greeting

By credit card, by mortgage renewal, by meagre savings
by bold and by brave and by luck and by will,

she should go.

Caravan

At Abkhazi Garden we drink Russian tea
that travelled across the Silk Road
in flat cakes: oolong, lapsang souchong,
chrysanthemum. My grandmother drank it,
holding sugar between her teeth to sweeten the leaves.
She had been a servant in my grandfather's house,
travelled with him to the New World.
Or so the story goes.
I watch the rhododendrons bloom.
There is nobody alive now
to confirm her story, none of her four sons,
her two daughters, her sisters. It is mine to embellish,
a history of pogrom and romance,
escape and rebirth. Happily ever after,
though my father told me years later
his mother confessed to him, *your father
doesn't love me anymore.* When would she tell him
such a thing? As they walked the buggy each Friday
before Shabbat, delivering the bootlegged liquor
she hid under the covers, money
to buy food for her children? As my father
helped her change the sheets in the boarders' rooms?
As she prepared another meal, cobbled together
from butcher scraps and vegetables from her garden?
Words reorganize the steps we take
from one day to the next. *Do you mean love
doesn't last?* my daughter had asked,
after I told her about the divorce to come.
Another story to embellish —
not years and years to grieve but a suitcase, a ticket,
an apartment in the seventh arrondissement.
From the flea market in Montmartre: two teacups
from Belarus, a large bronze samovar, oolong tea
in the late afternoon.

Psalm

I am standing on a bridge over the Malmö canal
on Rosh Hashanah, far from home. Behind me,
the flower markets of Lilla Torg Square, cafés
selling *kardemummabullar*, the sweet pastries
I eat every morning with oat milk and coffee.
Swans in the canal, jackdaws in the trees.
Everything the same and not the same.
The children in the playground speak English
to me, and I try out my few Swedish phrases
on shopkeepers, who respond in English too.
Near my daughter's apartment, the Malmö synagogue
keeps its doors locked, remembering swastikas
on building walls, the taunts of strangers.
I am not with my people on this holy day,
but I am with my family, pushing a stroller
down narrow streets, learning to fling
my prayers into the autumn wind,
thankful for what gifts are given on the tongue
and in the body, and I praise the cobblestones,
the wild pansies by the canal, and the mourning doves
cooing from the bushes in the park.
I praise the early twilight in this northern city,
and the late-morning sun, I praise a world
where night follows day and change
is the gift of loss, my daughter settling in
to her new home, and I praise the solstice
that reminds us, on the longest night,
that the light returns, all things return,
and I praise all the strollers
with small boys singing in them.

The Evening Phone Call

I catch her in between bites of dinner —
always macaroni and cheese, one chicken wing
(honey garlic), ice cream for dessert —
Hi sweetie, she says. I can hear her chew,
put down her fork, turn off the TV.
How was your day? I ask. Always good,
she tells me, I take my walk, do the shopping.
How was yours? She doesn't hear me,
doesn't listen either. Asks me again, how
was your day? The script needs to be simple,
or we will lose each other
in a labyrinth of words repeated
and distorted. She's a hundred,
her heart pumps faithfully, her lungs
breathe in and out without a pause,
even her knees work well. Each time we talk
I haul up a bucket of yesterdays, my tongue
stuck on stories I never completed, the ones
I need to mend, edit and rewrite.
Too late now, she doesn't remember
even the ones I just told her. She is content
to tell me about the morning's walk,
the three trees she sees from her window,
so much taller now, and how high will they grow?
And will everything end when they die?

Aubade at Amalfi

The boat has long gone
my friends wondering where I am
making up stories I am not in.

I am here with the jasmine and lemon,
you serve me *rigatoni*
with clams and artichoke.

Your feet against mine,
the intimacy of toes! Your shirt hangs
at the back of my chair.

We drink moments, we stretch time,
as if we could unwrinkle its curves and shallows,
its bells and buzzers.

You play some Elgar,
the slow Nimrod,
and then a *tarantella*. And I dance for you.

How you made me do it I don't know,
a red shawl around my hips,
and the hauberk, the gauntlets,

the weight of the armour I carry every day
now somewhere behind me,
heavy on the tiled floor of the patio.

When the sun rises, we will take the stairs
slowly, through the tunnels of the city,
the blue doors still asleep, and I will ride the dawn

to Naples. You will return to your cello,
strum each note I danced to,
the red shawl against your shoulders.

Öresund

Wind and cold rain, alone this Christmas,
remembering long-ago mornings
opening stockings, lumpy with gifts,
a poem taped to each wrapping —
gone now, except what I keep alive in memory.
My daughter decorates their Christmas tree
in Malmö, Sweden, while her son hugs the Christmas goat,
bought at Ikea. Lights along a dark street at 4 p.m.
aurora borealis above her.
It's all about light, these winter evenings,
fire in the grate, a lamp and a book.

And what are you doing now,
my grandson with the yellow curls
nobody wants to cut? Tucked into your mother's lap,
a story, a song, the pleasure
of crooning a baby to sleep. How to balance
joy and lonesomeness — one tinges the other
like the edges of cloud, the aftertaste
of coffee. My daughter's life in Sweden,
her boy growing up, one Lego block after another.
We choose the colours, or we let them arrive in our hands,
blindly moving through each moment.

Soon I will cross the narrow bridge, Copenhagen
to Malmö. I bless my daughter and her family,
and I bless their days as the days begin to lengthen,
the solstice blesses us with light, the past
warming us on this dark winter morning and
I will not fear, I tell myself.

Öresund: the bridge connecting Denmark to Sweden.

– III –

Walking the Dog

Just before dinner the street settles into twilight,
the shadows of the pines grow longer,

traffic filters through the privet hedges and clumps
of rhododendron. Roads slide into each other

like arms of a maze, but nobody's going anywhere —
just a stroll before dinner, the dog loping behind,

a man and a woman, heads down, talking through the day's
deeds. In a backyard, a girl and her brother,

still wearing the hot sun of midday, swipe at each other
with twigs and taunts. The man and woman pass me

on a street that curves around a rose garden,
fences climbing with clematis. We smile

as if we know each other, as if we are all
bungalow and small children and dog and supper

almost ready on the table and afternoons trimming the hedges
and mornings full of zippers and shoelaces

as if we all tied our smiles securely into place,
took them out on a leash, strolled along a twilight street

as if, behind our painted doors,
we had everything we ever thought we wanted.

My Father's Feet

Some things are a mystery: a billion billion galaxies,
the shape of a man's thoughts, a father's feet.

Did my mother hold those feet in her hand,
did she bend to kiss each toe?

Did she massage the day's weariness
from the instep, the heel, the long tendon of the ankle?

Did he slide his feet along her legs,
warmed them on long winter nights?

A daughter will bend, towel in hand,
wash the ankle, the tendons, the flattened veins —

wash the folds between each toe,
water dripping off the washcloth,

the yellow bowl, the soap,
the silence in the room broken by breath

held, released, held again, released.

My Mother's Wedding

My mother tells me she wore blue
to her wedding: "I wanted something practical,
that I could wear later," she said.
I imagine a pale, washed-sky chiffon,
yards of gathered fabric, though this is 1937.
She says her veil was "just a piece of gauze"
but I add lace at the edges, Belgian lace
and a circlet of pearls and small flowers.
I add a necklace, something my father
might have given her, if there had been money.
But there was a ring, blessings by the rabbi
and her reluctant father.
I see her through my father's eyes,
this beautiful young woman he has loved
since they were children: her laughter,
the way her head lies perfectly against his shoulder.
He loved her courage, her resilience, her impatience
to marry him. "Let's not wait any longer,"
she said and now there they were,
under the *chuppah*, a bouquet of white roses
and delphinium in her arms — something
her aunt might have given her from the garden.
Her hand in his, and under his feet
the smashed glass, the Temple destroyed and rebuilt,
their years ahead.

---

chuppah: the wedding canopy, under which the bride and groom stand.

Scripture

The zigzagged threads of the writing spider
slick with dew,
tangle of blackberry, like fingers
scritching across the rockery,
or the calligraphy of branches, winter trees
against a paper-grey sky:

These are ways to scribe a moment.

It's quiet now, at the centre of the web —
the golden strands stretched into syllables
scattered by wind, cuneiform made of silk
and memory — everything not yet said,
not yet written.

writing spider. in North America, the corn spider or zipper spider is sometimes
referred to as the writing spider because of the zigzag patterns of its web.

Shalom

after Naomi Shihab Nye's "Adios"

Coming or going, the word is the same:
arrive in peace, go in peace.
In the language of your neighbour,
the Arab family across the street
in Beer-sheva, Jerusalem,
the refugees arriving every day:
salaam. The root of the word
in the cells of that neighbour
some think of as your enemy.

What can a word do? Can you wear it
like a shawl? Use it like a shield?
Can you step into it
like your favourite pair of jeans?
Does it hurt your tongue
to say *shalom?*
Sing it — begin with sibilants,
end with a murmur —
the lilt of the "l" in the middle,
the wide vowels — open what can be opened,
close what must be closed.

Think of all the things that open:
black umbrellas in a summer rain,
the orchestra tuning up, violins
stretching the notes that begin
a Schubert quintet, a baby's eyes
gazing onto light, a mother's face.
Think of closings: a daisy at dusk,
the last night of your favourite play,
a book's final page. The end, the end,
a door shut on a marriage, a father's
last breath. *Shalom*: welcoming, letting go,
hands open for what might arrive next.

As If We Invented Love

We walked all night, past houses
with a window or two still lit,
past doorways and gates and a dog
that followed us for a while, then loped away.
Stars in the night sky, and we wished on each.
Everything new as if we invented love
and were polishing the gleam of it.
Toward dawn, a woman came out, stood by the door,
frowned at us. We grinned, wanting her to know
what it was like to love every single thing
we saw or heard or touched. Even her —
tumbled hair, old slippers, housecoat
wrapped grimly around her waist.
You bowed to her, I curtsied. She turned,
still grumbling, but I knew she was smiling.
I knew the leaves on the elm trees
jittered a little for our benefit. I knew,
in the ways only the young know
determined to make the world in their image,
we would walk down streets like this,
at midnight, at dawn, your arm on my shoulder,
walking stick in one hand,
eyeglasses glinting in the winter sun.

Boketto

I try to exist in the somehow, the might still be —
gaze upward to constellations of in-between.
— Susan Rich, "Boketto"

Boketto: *to stare out windows without purpose,*
the great pleasure of doing nothing, if you can stand it
and not torment yourself. That abundance of nothing
filled with attic rooms and lost children
and suitcases full of clothes
you've forgotten you had: the red Chinese sheath,
the green gown with the swirling skirt,
and how it felt, to spin, to glide,
to pull every eye to you. And do you remember
driving through the Fulford Valley,
the Bach cello suite on the radio,
and there was nothing more wonderful
than that moment — though your husband
had left you and the house was about to be sold.
Boketto, the hours drift by through other windows,
like the morning you sat in a *pousada* in Portugal,
outside, the olive trees in a silver herringbone field,
and where would we be without the spaces in between,
the pause between breaths, the backyard full of flickers
twitching out insects at the edge of the garden,
and the rain, drizzle or downpour,
the way it patterns the glass.

Vilna

Vilna, now Vilnius, where my grandfather lived as a boy,
before he became a rag man in Vancouver, calling from the
alleys of East Georgia and Keefer Street — before he met my
grandmother, before they hurt each other. I'll go back there,
reclaim what was lost, the shtetls that no longer exist, the
women with their bright kerchiefs, the kosher butcher shops,
the challah baker, the candle maker, the tiny synagogues where
the men swayed to Hebrew prayers. Here is my DNA, the parts
of me that sing in D minor, that fear the Holy Spirit, that long
for redemption — or at least something resembling joy. On the
cobbled streets of Vilna I will buy the chicken for the Sabbath
dinner, I will tuck the challah in my basket, I will smile at the
rabbi's son — I will erase all the years in between, follow my
grandfather back to the candles in the window, the Sabbath
Queen at the table, the wine in the cup.

Sliver of moon,
echoes of song through windows,
the white tablecloth.

Seventh Decade

i

Not a time for bikinis
or deep décolletage

nor red stiletto heels
crimson fingernails

There are no pheromones
seeking to fill the nursery

Many don't get to where you are, alive
and intact: eyes, ears, almost working knees

They fall by the wayside

or they forget the sudden joy of a small bird
perched on the branch of a lilac

in a corner of the garden, mostly weed
but holding, also, the perfect shape of a hydrangea

dried by a summer sun, delicate
and faintly blue.

ii

And why not stiletto heels?
someone's phone number tucked in a back pocket?

Nobody believes your age, anyway.
The elderly spinster, age seventy

with her baggy sweaters and crimped white hair,
a minor character in a British mystery novel.

Not you, surely. That villa by the sea,
yours still, if you want it.

The train ticket in your backpack,
the small village, the hike through the valley,

and here, in the palm of your hand,
one flawed crystal, reflecting the huge sky.

Tashlik

Bottom of the hill from Dallas Road,
stone steps that curve around Garry oak
and blackberry, broom and bluegrass,
down to a small beach, once a midden.
Selach lanu, forgive us our trespasses.
We are there with the Coast Salish
and with our European ancestors,
our hands full of stones.

Begin here — this stretch of ocean,
flotsam of plastic rings and beer cans
scattered among the driftwood, the carapace of crabs.
Clean the shoreline as you rinse the longing from your hands.
Remember the plastic island the size of Texas
floating in the middle of the bright Pacific.

Sound of the sea, sound of *shofars* blowing
tekiah, teruah, shevarim. A frisson down the spine.
Forgive the knives we have held in our hands,
our upraised arms, fisted. Forgive our words
and our silence. Forgive the paths we are afraid to take,
our wrong directions. I throw my stone,
the one that has sat on my desk all year,
collecting the deeds I wish undone
the ones I should have completed.

Cast your sins upon the water, says the prophet.
Walk along the shore, listen to the rhythm of waves,
the scent of seaweed, the cry of gull and cormorant.
Gather the kelp to feed your gardens —
offer kale, lettuce, squash and zucchini for the hungry
who line up at the food bank, fill the temporary shelters.
The waves thrum like a heartbeat, *tshuvah,* return.
A fist against the heart, *selach lanu.*

Tashlik: a tradition on the first day of Rosh Hashanah, to cast stones into the sea.

Selach lanu: "Forgive us," part of the Jewish High Holiday prayers.

tekiah, teruah, shevarim: the three notes played by the shofar on the High Holidays.

Aubade to Father

Your lips are dry — I dab them with a sponge,
careful not to bother you with gesture.
They said you would die tonight so I sit,
curled in a blanket by your side.
I want you not to be alone, want to be
witness to your leaving. My hand in yours,
fingers on your heartbeat — that moment.
I want to be there.

What are you listening to? I used to ask you,
your headphones, in the quiet, and you gave me
what had pleased you. Tonight, it is Mozart
and Elgar, melodies you loved.

A daughter's love — wordless, a shape
she holds against every man she meets,
wanting what her mother had — no, not quite.
As I said, wordless.

I stumble when I speak. Try to tell you,
dutifully, that it is all right for you to leave.
Yevarechecha — the blessing you gave me then.
Bless me now, father, stay a little longer. Let death
be for other people. Sing to me, the morning sun
on your white hair, the first birds.

Walking the Seawall

One heron on a sandbar, low tide,
lifting of the spirit
from belly to heart to a catch in the throat

like those days in the mirrored room,
the wooden barre along three sides
the thrill of percussion along the veins:
plié, bend, turn, stretch.

A slide of light through grey cloud,
rays of light like fingers, pebbles of light
on the water. In front of me, blue sky,

behind me, dark clouds over the far hills.
Nothing has changed except this lifting
which changes everything.

Be Ready for the Third Day

Let them be ready for the third day,
for on the third day the Lord will come down,
in the sight of all the people, on Mount Sinai.

— Exodus 19:11

On the first day,
I hide in the wilderness,
hard black stones burdening my pocket.
I name these stones: Deadly Resistance
Lazybones Know-Nothing
Waster of Precious Time.
One more episode on Netflix,
one more bag of chips, a Coke, a whiskey.
Let me sleep, let me dream.
I cannot not hold the pen, the brush,
the flute. I am not worthy.

On the second day, I begin,
though my mind wanders, distracted by bird and bread
and the ache in my knees.
I pace the room, stare at the blank page
as if staring would make pencils
of my eyes. *Write or die* I tell myself,
but the words, like children, have run out of the classroom,
they are frolicking on the hills,
they will not come back.

I am not worthy, *Hashem*, choose someone else.

We are just ordinary people.
Our best intentions fade a month after the New Year —
the morning walks, the few minutes of meditation,
the mumbled prayers. A moment's sweat,
breathe in, breathe out, all we can give.
How shall we endure the face of God?

On the third day
I dress in clean white robes,
wash my feet in a yellow bowl,
walk barefoot towards the mountain.
I wait, with the others.
A pillar of fire, a cloud, a voice.
We cry out, and fall down on our faces.
Lord, we are unworthy. How shall we endure?

And when I rise, what then?
Will my blood flow differently? Will my eyes
see what I have not seen before,
some veil lifted, some molecules
rearranged? Will I see the *yesh* of things,
the thisness? Or will nothing have changed,
but the seeing of it?

The fire in the cloud, the smell of thunder,
the light.

I will build a Tabernacle in my heart.
I will mend the broken stones with gold,
fill the cracks in the yellow bowl,
place it on the altar. I will pick up the pen,
the brush, the flute.
Do my work.

Hashem: a substitute name for God.

I will build a Tabernacle in my heart: rabbinical interpretation of Exodus.

Berlin

The U-Bahn, the S-Bahn, the Ringbahn, the trams, the
buses. Everything connects, in a city where years ago nothing
connected. East Berlin, the Wall, and before that, Kristallnacht,
the Nuremburg Laws, the trucks, the trains. It was sunny, and
then it rained. In the Neues Museum, the bust of Nefertiti,
the Ishtar Gate, the Aleppo Room: disconnected tiles pieced
together, what once was. On the banks of the Spree River, deck
chairs sprawled, beer and music and in an alleyway, a cellist
plays "Lara's Theme," a man invites a woman to dance. Between
the tall coffins of the Memorial to Murdered Jews, teenagers
hide and kiss. "In Berlin you can get anything you want, at any
time," the taxi driver tells me. What do I want? In the Jewish
Museum, a room, high walls without windows, oddly angled, a
sliver of light at the top of one wall. Where is the door? Is it
locked? Where is the way out? Dread deep in the marrow.

Who walked below my feet?
Stumble on stones. Labyrinth.
Hold onto the flame.

Still Life with Small Boy

One red tablecloth, two wooden chairs,
a table beside a window. A small boy,
swinging his legs, a cup of hot chocolate.
A woman leans toward him, her grey hair
lit from the late sun. She dips a spoon
into his cup. "Bubby don't do that!" he protests,
and she gives him a bit of her croissant.
Heads together, bending into each other.
They are a world. Outside, the world breaks.
She cannot read the news while she is with him,
tries to be calm, listens while he tells her
his new red bike helmet makes him safe.
He shows her the helmet, puts it on. "Look,"
he says. "Safe."
                    "Have more chocolate," she tells him.

Saturday in Trastevere

I drink orzo cappuccino in Café Markesa
in Trastevere, Rome. Ivy climbs the pink walls
and the sun gleams on the cobblestones.
I watch and listen and write.

In Trastevere ivy climbs the walls
and music of a wedding in the church next door.
Look and listen and write the day.
The woman beside me frowns: another *tourista*.

A wedding, a church organ, a Bach cantata.
The bride and groom kneel, murmur prayers.
The woman beside me, frowning, reads her paper.
I am a few seconds in someone's life.

Murmur of prayers, buzz of summer flies.
I am invisible in the corridors of the church.
A few seconds in someone's life,
they, a small story in mine.

Invisible, but the visible world chants a blessing,
greens the walls of ancient buildings.
I am a small story: frowning woman, kneeling bride,
a man on the bus this morning whistled Mozart.

Ivy on the ancient walls, begonias in the planters,
the sun on the cobblestones.
We are small stories in each other's lives,
as I drink orzo cappuccino in Café Markesa.

Happiness

Even when they came back from the desert,
their hair full of sand, their eyes hollow, even then,
at the end of the far stretches of dune,
there was a flower:
bright crimson centre like a beating heart,
white petals blazing in the sun
                    beside the ruined temple.

Isaac

Ishmael, I have come to you
after my father tried to kill me. Our father.
He said he was going to pray. He said
it was as it should be. He took a knife.

Ishmael, he sent you away, into the desert,
you and your mother. And now,
I see the fields around you,
green, with vineyards and olive trees.
Your sons till the soil, your daughters
fill the kitchen with the smell of rosemary.

Work follows grief, a garden built
from seeds plucked from the desert.

Today I walked from Moriah. I remember
the point of his knife so near my skin I could feel
its heat. Can still hear the voice,
Abraham Abraham, do not kill your son.
Would he have, I wonder. He untied me,
his eyes on the stones beneath his feet. I turned away.

Ishmael, my brother. The blood of our father
stains us both.

Moriah: the mountain where Abraham almost sacrificed his son Isaac,
doing God's bidding. It is thought that Isaac joined his brother Ishmael
after this incident.

Four a.m.

Not even the day shift of crow and rooster.
The hour of Lauds, the Dawn Prayer.
Psalms that begin, "oh no"

and "please" and "too late."
Get up? or try to convince yourself to sleep?
Inhale, exhale, empty the mind

of its antiquated ruminations.
Hum the cantatas you once listened to.
Recite each port

your ship anchored at,
the rocking against the ropes.
The slope of the land, the night sky

split with stars. Light creeps dawnward
and still the panoply of doubts, like the line of kings
the witches promised Banquo. We sleep no more.

The rook, the raven, the nightjar
flap the darkness into light
too slowly. Itches, scratches, flayed flesh.

This serrated morning,
dim-shadowed, blood-washed.
the murdered days behind the door.

Wabi-Sabi

Her favourite coffee mug, cobalt blue,
cracked one morning in their new home.
Her husband advised her to throw it out.
She could not fill the break with gold,
in the *kintsugi* method. When she poured
mocha java and steamed milk together
the way it was done in Portugal,
the cup neither spilled nor leaked nor nicked her lip.
Sitting alone at the table each morning,
she admired the way the crack meandered
across the glaze, caught the light.

Wabi-sabi: Japanese word indicating appreciation for the old, the worn,
the not-perfect.

Take Care of Your Mother

after Li Young Lee's "Moon from Any Window"

In the last shreds of a dream
my father tells me,
Take care of your mother.

I know three things. One:
I'll never learn the trick of being a tree.

Two: A daughter is three birds and four winds,
and the three birds have her mother's beak
and her father's wings

or maybe she's a mountain stream
and the mountains where she begins
are covered in ice and meadows
or is she only the leaves drifting on the water?

When the clouds become mirrors
and show me what I need to do
for my mother, I remember three things.
One: a father's love

is winter soup,
one part grief and two parts laughter,
and what's left over fills the room
with singing. Prayers and praises.

And patience, that's the bridge hand
my father laid out every morning,
berating his silent partner.

And wisdom? That's the leaves
bending with the wind, falling and blossoming
in the rain and sun

When the morning asks,
Have you taken care of your mother?
I know there is no place

I can bury my sorrow.
I know the caves on the mountainside
are the earth's desire to dream
and its need to open itself to possibility

and my sorrow is a gift
from a stranger, with a message
written on the same parchment
my father reads from.

My father asks,
have you done what I asked?
And are you happy now?

A troubled daughter. A father
in the wind. The clouds gathering.

Balance

Long days of moments, random
and not unhappy. Days without desire.

Who wouldn't guess I chose
this life? The quiet. The red maple

outside the room. The one rose
on the neglected bush. Each morning

the hummingbird sits on the branch
and the blackberry tangles itself around the trunk.

It is easy to dawdle through the day
remembering other days: ferry schedules

and traffic, delayed dinners and morning alarms,
papers piled on the desk, waiting.

Slowly understanding this balance —
not each side in equilibrium

but first one then its opposite.
First fast and then slow. First

together now apart. The gradual
knowing that this is good. The cat

moving across the lawn, pausing
to catch my eye. The pen

pausing in mid-air. The life of the mind.
Eyes outward and inward, flexing

the stretched hour.

Known and Strange Things

> *You are neither here nor there,*
> *A hurry through which known and strange things pass*
> *As big soft buffetings come at the car sideways*
> *And catch the heart off guard and blow it open.*
> — Seamus Heaney, "Postscript"

You sit in a café in the city where you live, your usual
latte and scone. A cloudy Sunday morning, August,
a blank page. Anything can happen. Or nothing.
You are not on anyone's calendar, though the city
is full of things to do, if you wish it. A flamenco dance
in the city square, a protest march through the streets.
Your thoughts full of trains and planes, visas,
hotels. Timetables to get you elsewhere,
Amsterdam or Malmö, Stockholm or Rome.
You are neither here nor there

not in Sweden with your family,
nor fully here, at this café, where the leaves on the patio
are brown with too much sun, and the morning opens slowly.
Your life is a question without an answer.
Colours on a palette, alizarin blends into citron,
yellow softens the red, builds the image you paint:
sand and sea and one dog at the water's edge.
Take it slow, your eyes a paintbrush,
follow the rhythm of tide and driftwood, not
a hurry through which known and strange things pass

like your planned trip through Europe,
hustle through Germany, a brief pause
in Prague, on and on as the train gulps the miles,
so much so fast, and where are you? only a glimpse
in passing, farmhouse and garden, red tiled roofs
against green hills, blue mountains in the distance.
Somewhere in a village in Italy a man plays his flute,
a woman kneads bread. A vineyard, a woodshed,
a trace of jasmine through the open train window,
As big soft buffetings come at the car sideways.

What do you want, at this tail end of your life.
What is still possible? Nerves tense, muscles tight
in the early hours of morning. You stand at the window,
your mind in Sweden, your body rooted here.
The years put down layers, like rings of a tree,
like paint thickening with each brush stroke,
reds browning and blues blackening,
and what will it take to scrape the canvas clean,
open the coves of yellow, the light? Unfist the hand,
catch the heart off guard and blow it open.

You Could

There is a white room
the size of a cage —
two steps forward, stumble.
Two steps sideways, crash.
Easier to crouch
in the centre. Keep still.
The walls are vinegar white,
fire white. Easier to squint,
make the eyes a closed fist.

On the wall behind you is a door,
nail-studded, heavy oak, barred
and padlocked. There is no key.
There is no way, that way.
No air seeps from beneath,
no light crawls from above.
Not even the memory
of what the door hides
has room here.

It takes weeks to see the window,
days more to open the shutters,
wooden too but sun-bleached.
The curtain is translucent,
it moves in a hidden breeze.
Outside there is sunlight, a path,
a few stray grasses elbowing the rubble.
You hear sounds of children
though you still curl like a pillbug
in the middle of the room.

You could be there, you could
climb out the window, but that is not
a thing you do. You wait
on wooden slats of floor
cursing your knees.

There is another door.
How did you miss it? Neither locked
nor barred nor any spells
cast on it. Not a small Alice door,
but white, like the room.
Almost invisible. You could open it,
if you wish. You could
place one foot outside,
walk onto the stone path.
You could take a breath of the rose-filled air.
You could join the children,
your hands against the cold metal links of the swing.
You could lean back, pump your legs,
push yourself forward, back, forward.
You could almost fly.

ABOUT THE AUTHOR

Barbara Pelman is a poet and a retired English teacher who has taught at high schools and universities. An assistant and occasional host at Planet Earth Poetry, she also teaches poetry workshops. She has two books of poetry: *One Stone* (Ekstasis Editions, 2005) and *Borrowed Rooms* (Ronsdale Press, 2008), and a chapbook *Aubade Amalfi* (Rubicon Press, 2016). She is a frequent visitor to Sweden, where her family now lives. Barbara makes her home in Victoria, British Columbia.

MARQUIS

Québec, Canada